The Periodic Table of Elements

Post-Transition Metals, Metalloids and Nonmetals

Children's Chemistry Book

BABY PROFESSOR

EDUCATION KIDS

In this book, we are going to cover the Periodic Table of Elements. We're also going to take an in-depth look at Post-Transition Metals, Metalloids, and Nonmetals. So let's dive right in!

WHAT IS THE PERIODIC TABLE OF ELEMENTS?

The Periodic Table is called "periodic" because its elements are organized in periods, also called cycles. The elements are organized in rows by their atomic number, which indicates the number of protons that each element has in its nucleus.

Periodic Table of Elements

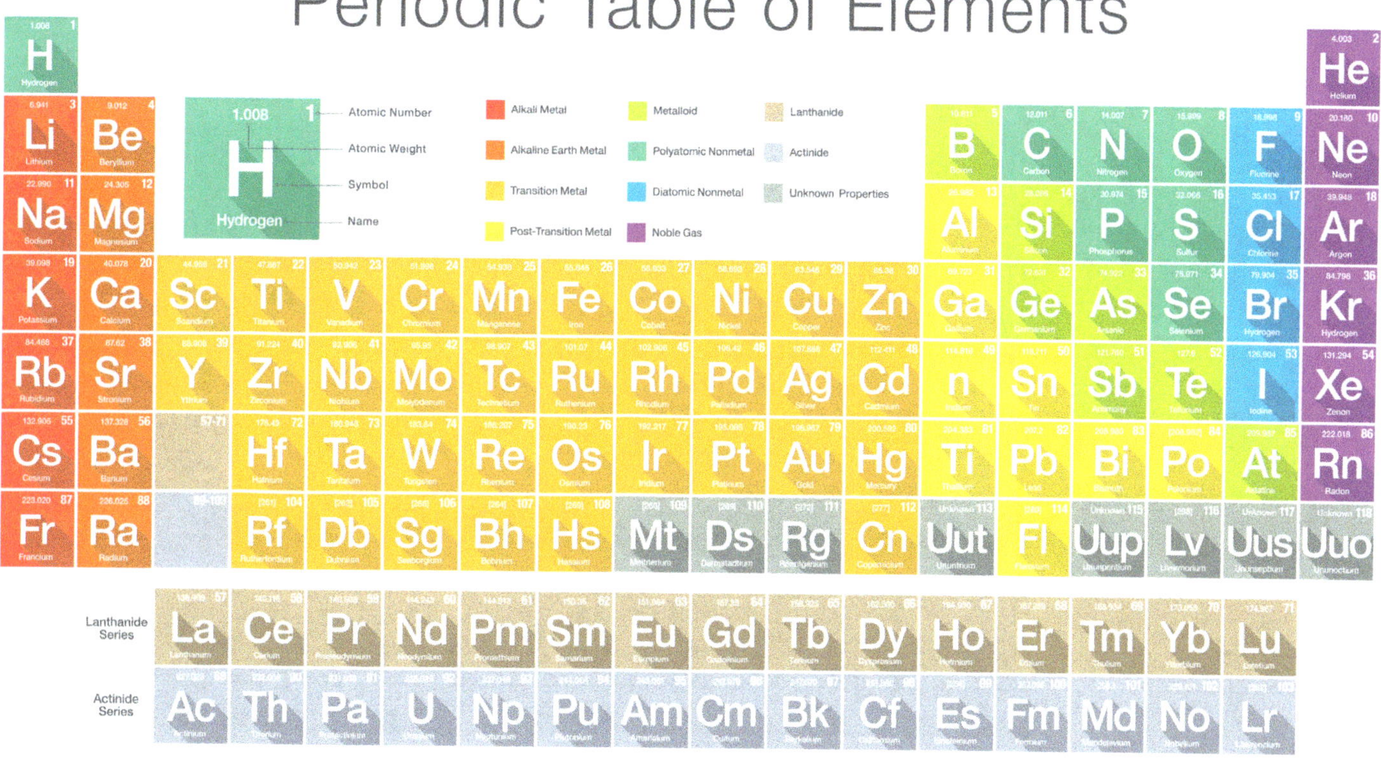

The Periodic Table of the Elements

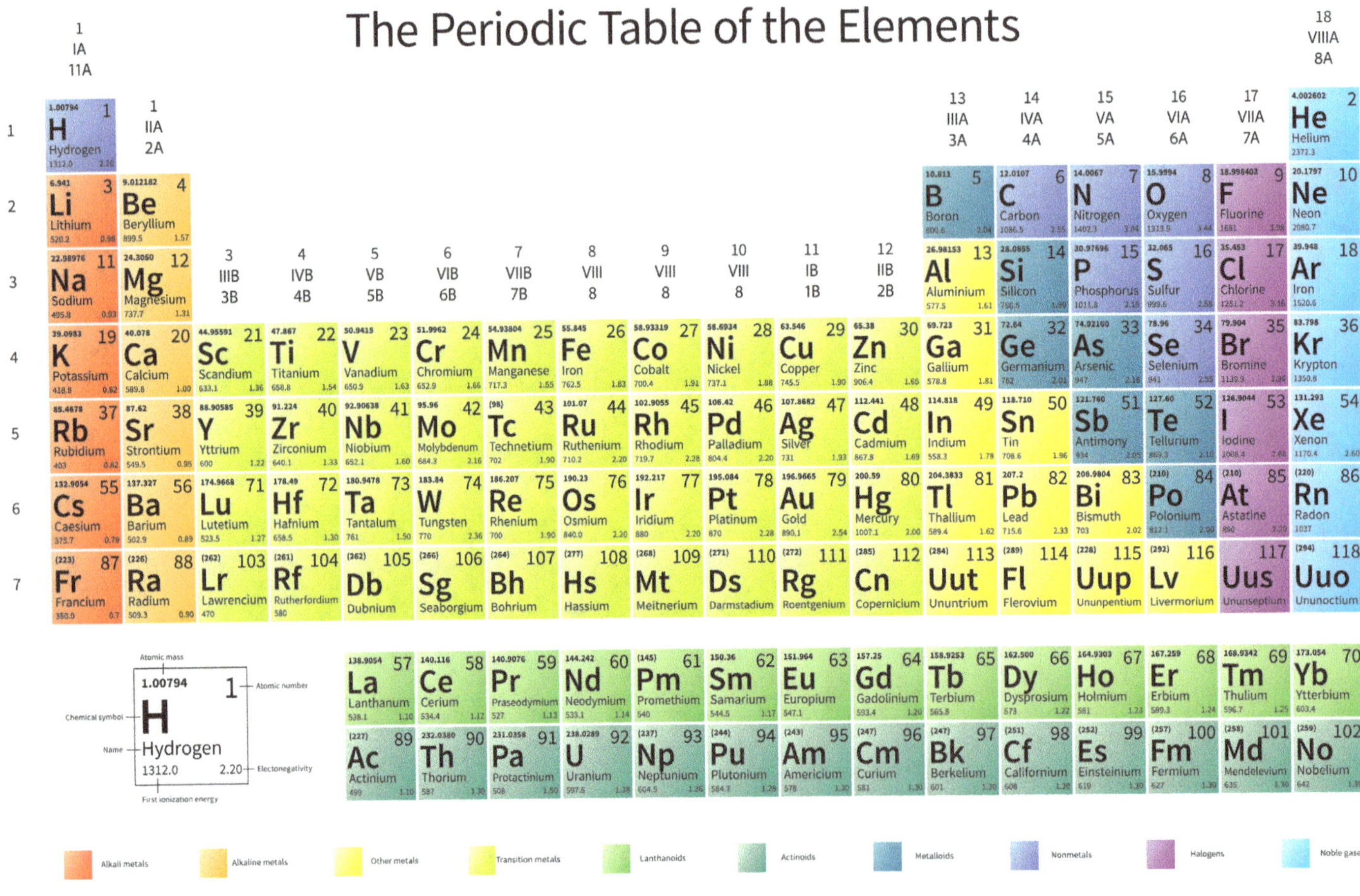

You'll notice when you look at the Periodic Table that some columns are skipped. This is so that the elements that have valence electrons of exactly the same number align on the same columns.

Valence electrons are electrons that can create chemical bonds, so they are important to the element's properties. Lined up in this way in columns, these elements have some properties that are similar. Each of the horizontal rows in the Periodic Table is called a period.

Periodic Table

OF ELEMENTS

1	2	3	4	5	6	7	8	9	10	11	12	13	14	15	16	17	18
H																	He
Li	Be											B	C	N	O	F	Ne
Na	Mg											Al	Si	P	S	Cl	Ar
K	Ca	Sc	Ti	V	Cr	Mn	Fe	Co	Ni	Cu	Zn	Ga	Ge	As	Se	Br	Kr
Rb	Sr	Y	Zr	Nb	Mo	Tc	Ru	Rh	Pd	Ag	Cd	In	Sn	Sb	Te	I	Xe
Cs	Ba	57-71	Hf	Ta	W	Re	Os	Ir	Pt	Au	Hg	Tl	Pb	Bi	Po	At	Rn
Fr	Ra	89-105	Rf	Db	Sg	Bh	Hs	Mt	Ds	Rg	Cn	Uut	Fl	Uup	Lv	Uus	Uuo

Lanthanide Series

La	Ce	Pr	Nd	Pm	Sm	Eu	Gd	Tb	Dy	Ho	Er	Tm	Yb	Lu
57	58	59	60	61	62	63	64	65	66	67	68	69	70	71

Actinide Series

Ac	Th	Pa	U	Np	Pu	Am	Cm	Bk	Cf	Es	Fm	Md	No	Lr
89	90	91	92	93	94	95	96	97	98	99	100	101	102	103

Periodic Table of Elements

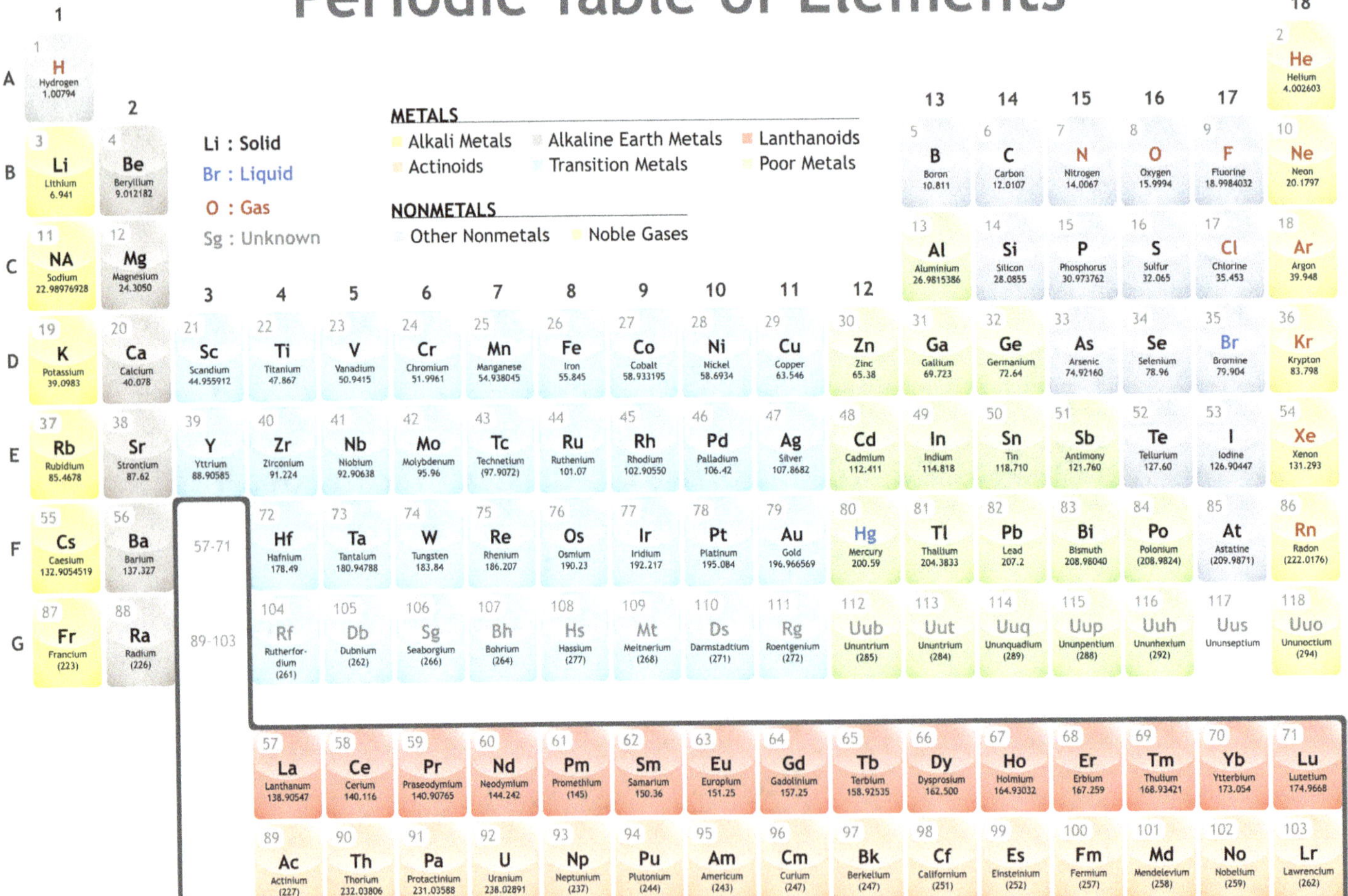

HOW MANY PERIODS DOES THE TABLE HAVE?

The entire table is considered to have either seven or eight periods, with the first period being short. The first period only contains the elements of hydrogen and helium. The sixth period of the table has 32 elements.

As you travel across the row from left to right, the element that is at the very left in the row has only 1 electron in its outer shell. The element at the very right has a full shell of electrons.

★ ★ Periodic Table Of The Elements ★ ★

Metals
- Alkali Metals
- Alkaline Earth Metals
- Actinoids
- Lanthanoids
- Transition Metals
- Poor Metals

Nonmetals
- Other Nonmetals
- Noble Gases

GROUP / PERIOD	1a	2a	3b	4b	5b	6b	7b	8	8	8	1b	2b	3a	4a	5a	6a	7a	0
1	H																	He
2	Li	Be											B	C	N	O	F	Ne
3	Na	Mg											Al	Si	P	S	Cl	Ar
4	K	Ca	Sc	Ti	V	Cr	Mn	Fe	Co	Ni	Cu	Zn	Ga	Ge	As	Se	Br	Kr
5	Rb	Sr	Y	Zr	Nb	Mo	Tc	Ru	Rh	Pd	Ag	Cd	In	Sn	Sb	Te	I	Xe
6	Cs	Ba		Hf	Ta	W	Re	Os	Ir	Pt	Au	Hg	Tl	Pb	Bi	Po	At	Rn
7	Fr	Ra	89-103** Actinides	Rf	Db	Sg	Bh	Hs	Mt	Ds	Rg							

*Lanthanides: La, Ce, Pr, Nd, Pm, Sm, Eu, Gd, Tb, Dy, Ho, Er, Tm, Yb, Lu

**Actinides: Ac, Th, Pa, U, Np, Pu, Am, Cm, Bk, Cf, Es, Fm, Md, No, Lr

WHY ARE THE GROUPS IN THE PERIODIC TABLE IMPORTANT?

Just as periods are the rows of the table, groups are the table's columns. There are 18 groups in the table and each group has different properties. For example, one group of elements is the noble gases, which are also called inert gases.

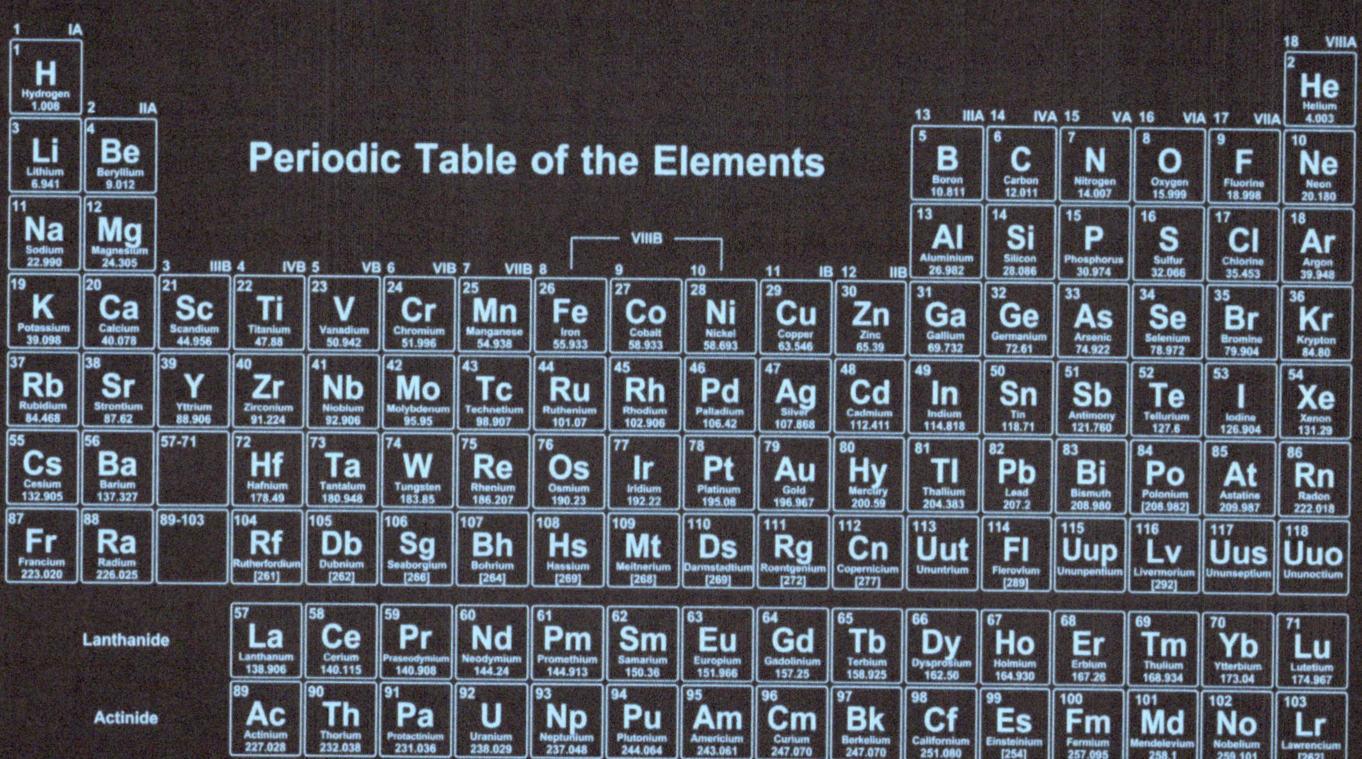

Periodic Table of the Elements
Lanthanide
Actinide

Periodic Table of Elements

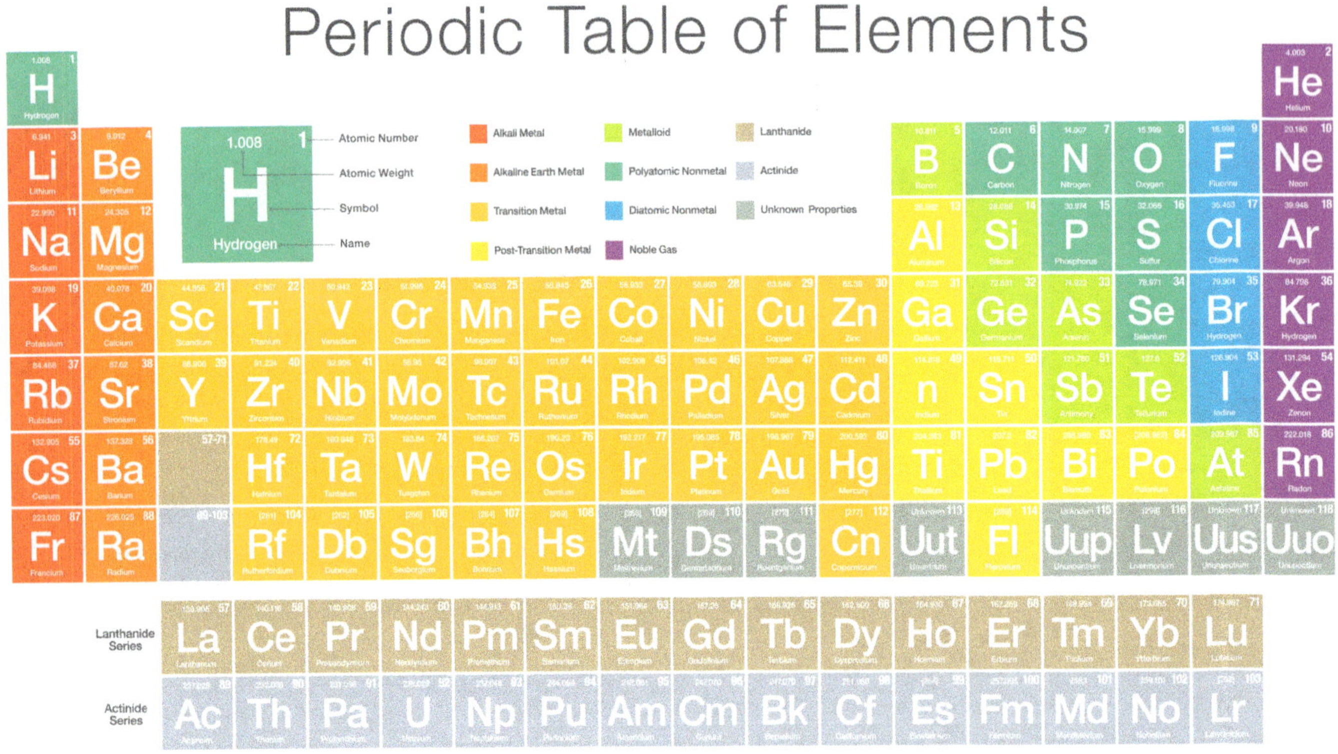

The inert gases all line up in the last column of the table. Because of their full outer shell of electrons, these gases are very stable, which simply means that under most circumstances they don't react with other elements.

Another example of grouped elements is the alkali metals. Aligned in the very left column, these elements all have only 1 electron in their outer shells. This means that they are very reactive, which means they are unstable and react quickly with other elements, unlike the noble gases.

PERIODIC TABLE OF THE ELEMENTS

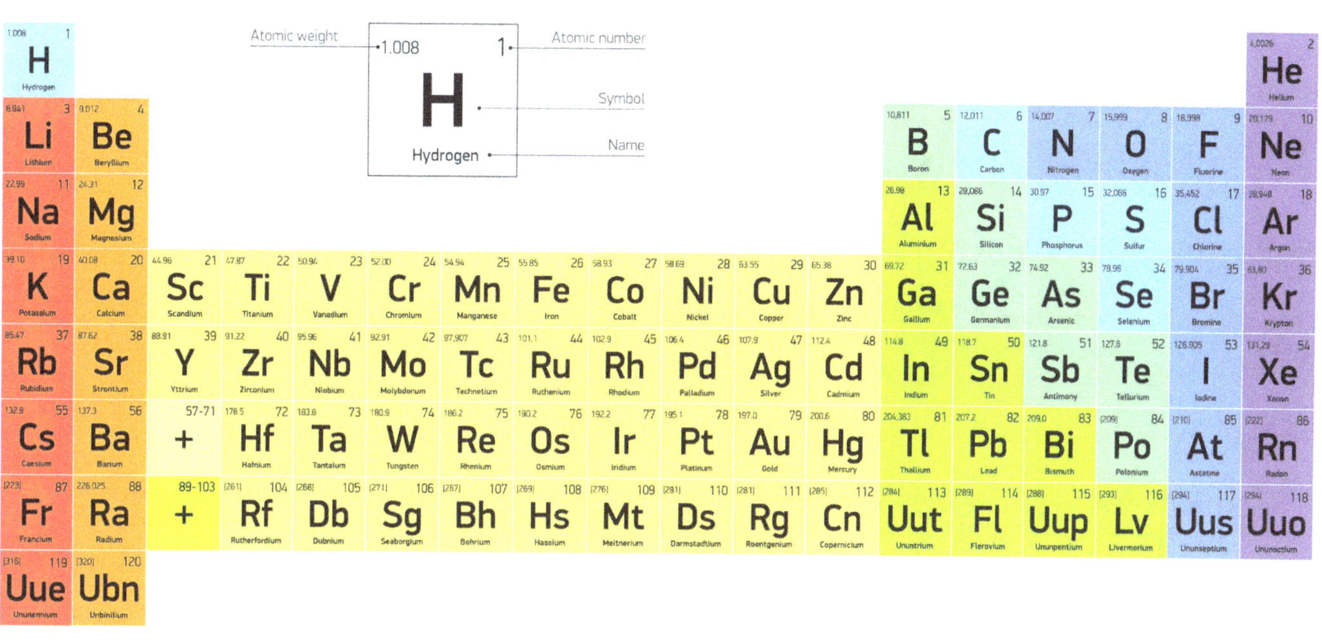

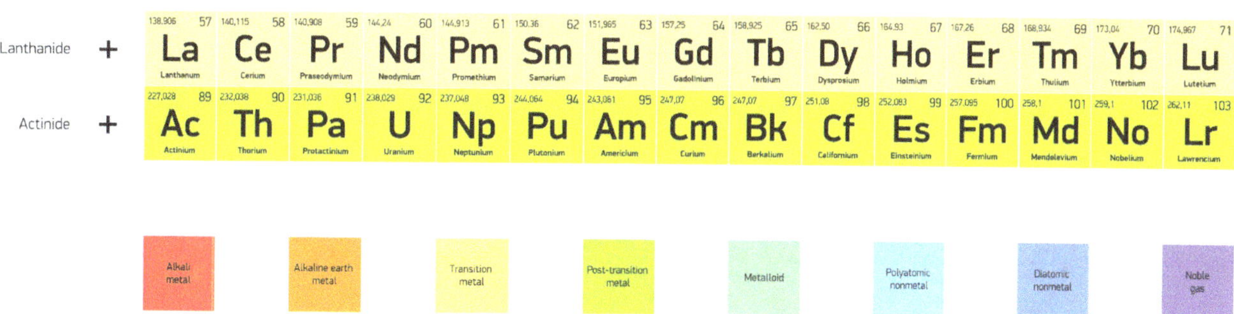

Periodic Table of Elements

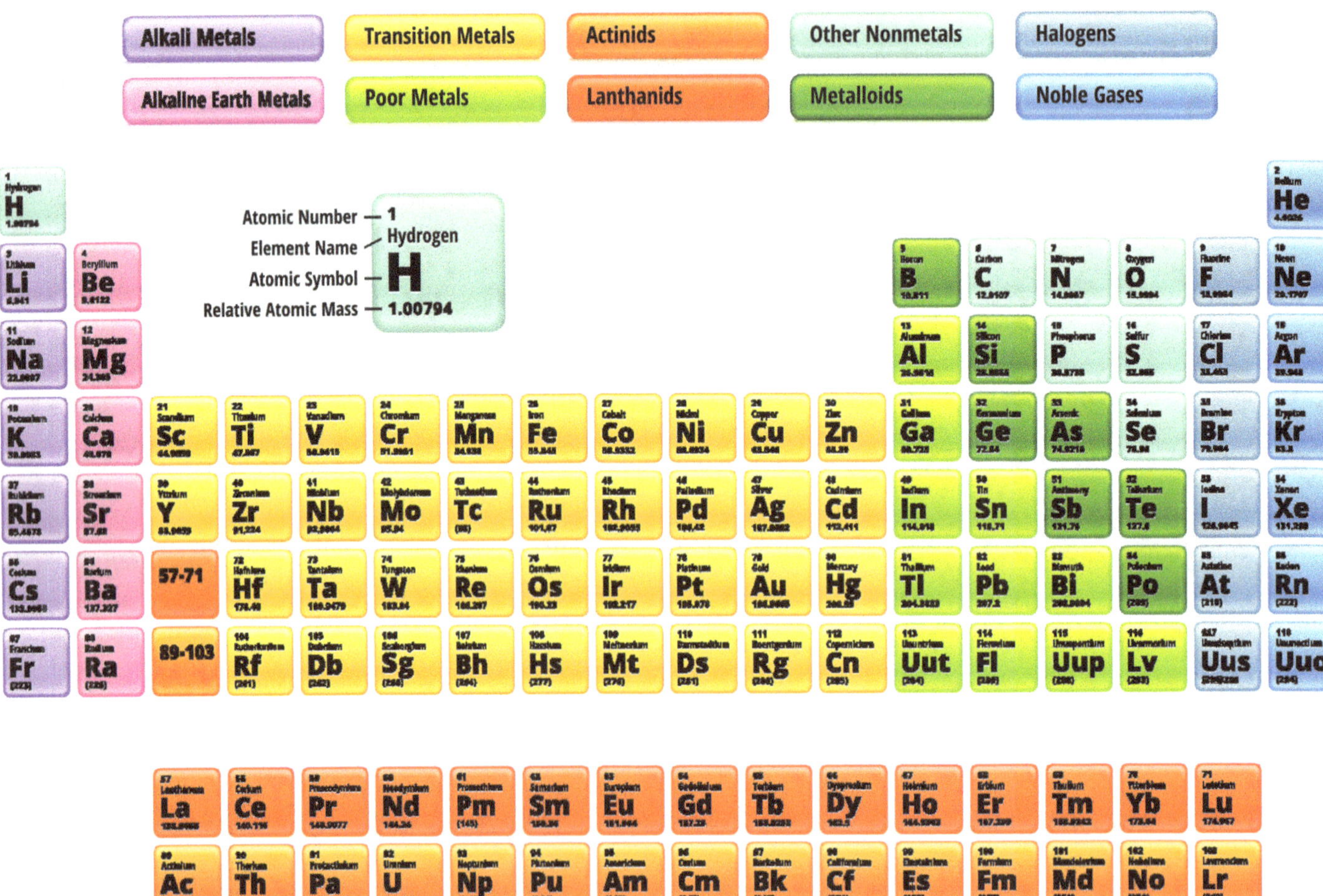

Chemists can use the periodic table to interpret whether a particular element might react or what properties it has, by studying the way groups are organized.

ABBREVIATIONS FOR THE ELEMENTS

The periodic table contains abbreviations that represent the names of the elements. Some abbreviations are easy to remember since they are a shortened version of the element's name, like HE for Helium.

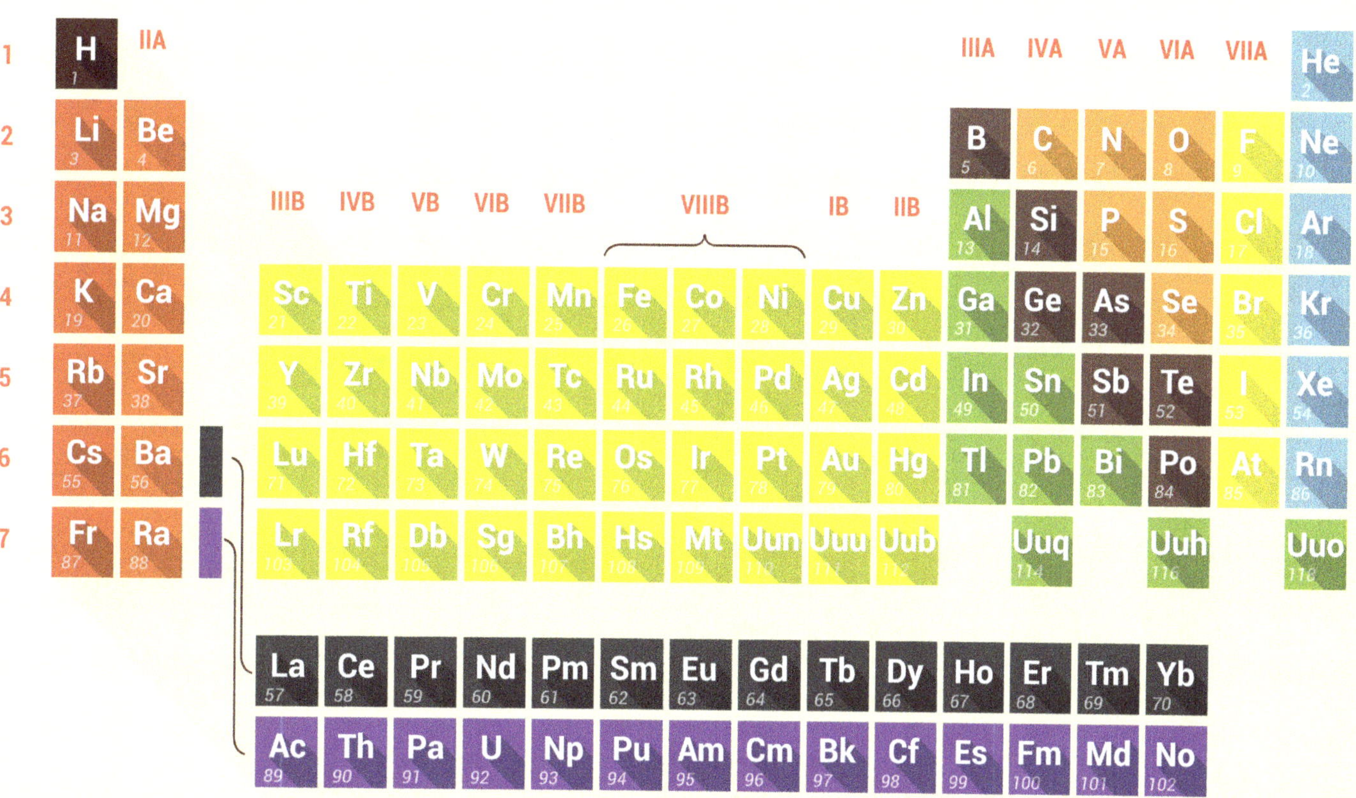

PERIODIC TABLE

group

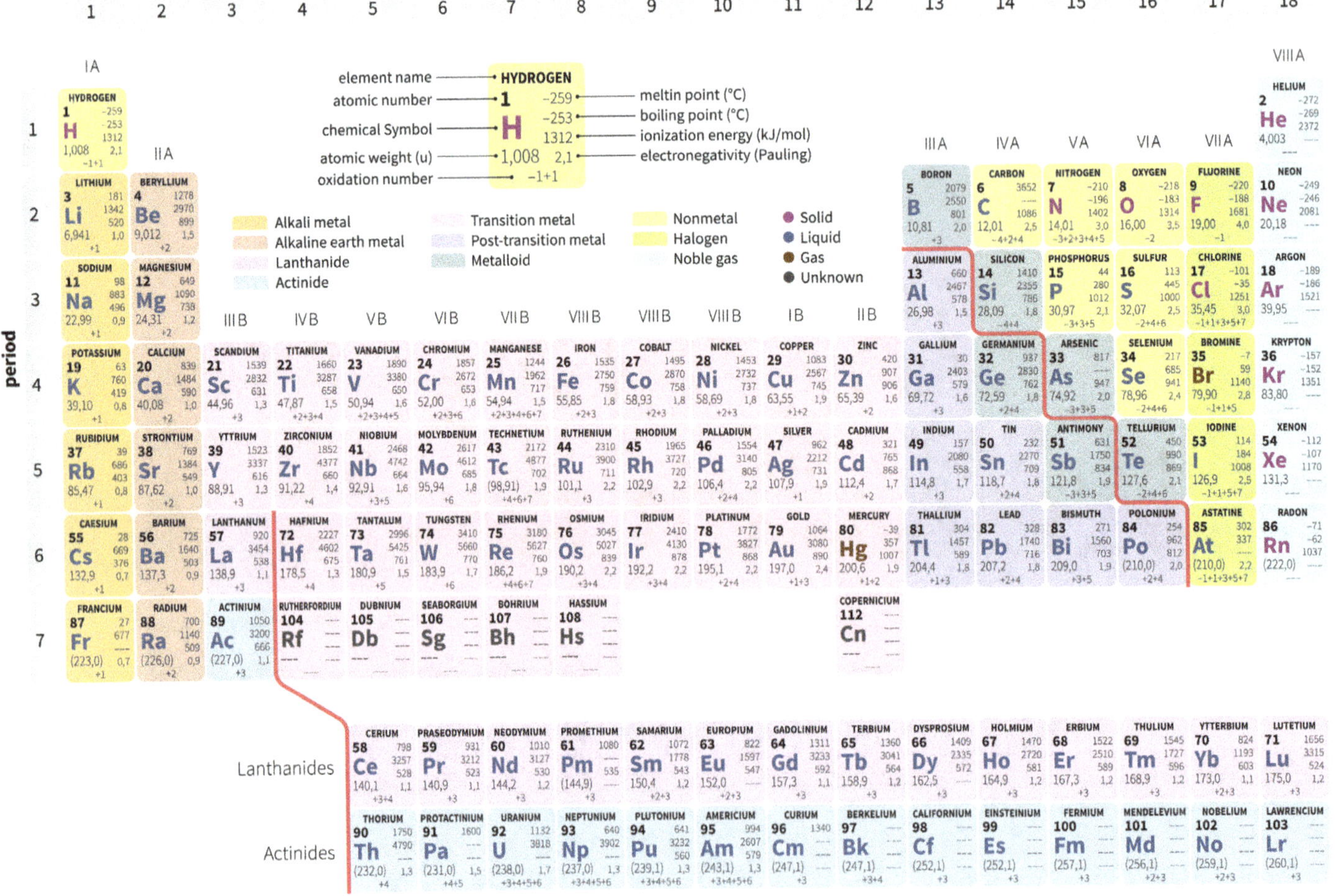

However, some of them are based on Latin words, such as "Au," which stands for the Latin word for gold, which is "aurum." The abbreviation for the element of Iron comes from the Latin word for Iron, which is "ferrum."

WHO INVENTED THE PERIODIC TABLE?

In 1869, Dmitri Mendeleev, a chemist in Russia, first proposed a way of organizing the elements. At that time, not all the elements had been discovered. By organizing them the way he did, he was able to predict some properties of elements that had not yet been found.

D.I. MENDELEJEW
1834–1907
40 GR
POLSKA
ST.CZ. CHLUDZINSKI   PWPW   E. KONECKI SC.

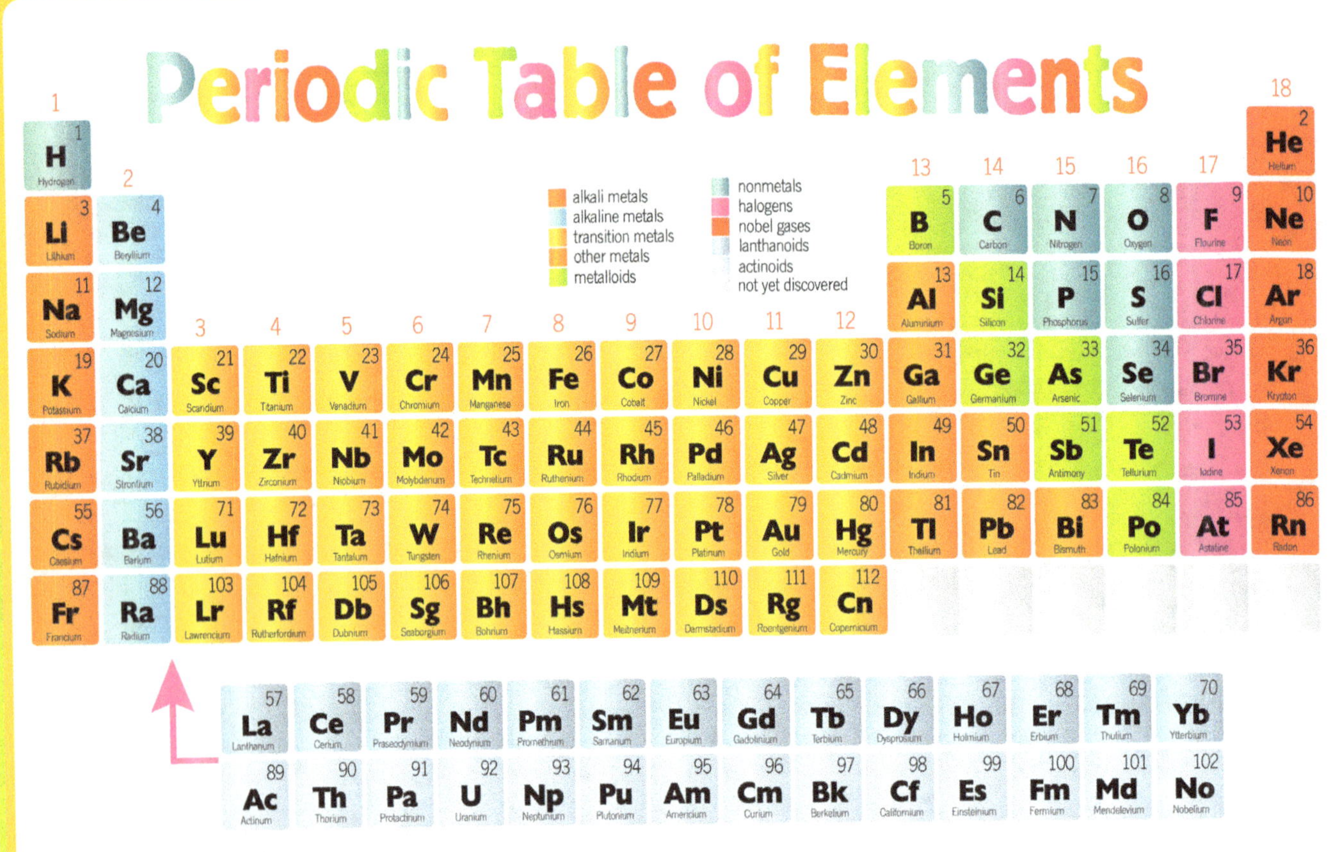

Periodic Table of Elements
alkali metals
alkaline metals
transition metals
other metals
metalloids
nonmetals
halogens
nobel gases
lanthanoids
actinoids
not yet discovered

FUN FACTS ABOUT THE PERIODIC TABLE

• There wouldn't be any life on Earth without the element of carbon. It's known to form at least 10 million different types of compounds. Carbon is abundant everywhere, unlike the element of francium, which is the rarest element on the face of planet Earth. At any given period of time, there are only a few ounces.

• If you look carefully you'll see that all the letters of the alphabet, except for the letter J, are used in the table.

• The element of helium, represented by HE in the table, exists on Earth, but was first discovered during observations of the sun.

• It would be difficult to figure out which element Ag stands for. In Latin, the word for silver is "argentum." It's easier to remember that the abbreviation Ag stands for silver, if you remember that the country of Argentina is named after this Latin word because of its huge silver deposits.

POST-TRANSITION METALS

Themetalsthatareconsideredtobepost-transition are located between those labeled transition and those labeled metalloids. Scientists can't come to an agreement about this group. In addition to being labeled "post-transition," they are sometimes referred to as "other" metals or "poor" metals.

10.811
1s² 2s² 2p
8.29980
13
Al
2P°
1/2
Aluminum
26.981538
[Ne]3s² 3p
5.9858
31
Silico
28.08
[Ne
2P°

aluminium **Al** 13		
gallium **Ga** 31		
indium **In** 49	tin **Sn** 50	
thallium **Tl** 81	lead **Pb** 82	bismuth **Bi** 83

WHICH ELEMENTS ARE POST-TRANSITION METALS?

What to name these elements isn't the only confusion! Chemists don't agree about which metals belong in this group either. Typically, the 13th, 14th, and 15th groups are organized here. These elements are aluminum, bismuth, gallium, indium, thallium, tin, and lead. The element of polonium is frequently grouped with them.

WHAT ARE THE PROPERTIES OF THE METALS LABELED POST-TRANSITION?

Under most conditions, post-transition metals are malleable, which means they can be molded. They are also ductile, which means they aren't brittle. They're also good conductors of both heat as well as electricity. They are fairly high in density, but they are softer than the transition metals. They also have lower melting as well as lower boiling points.

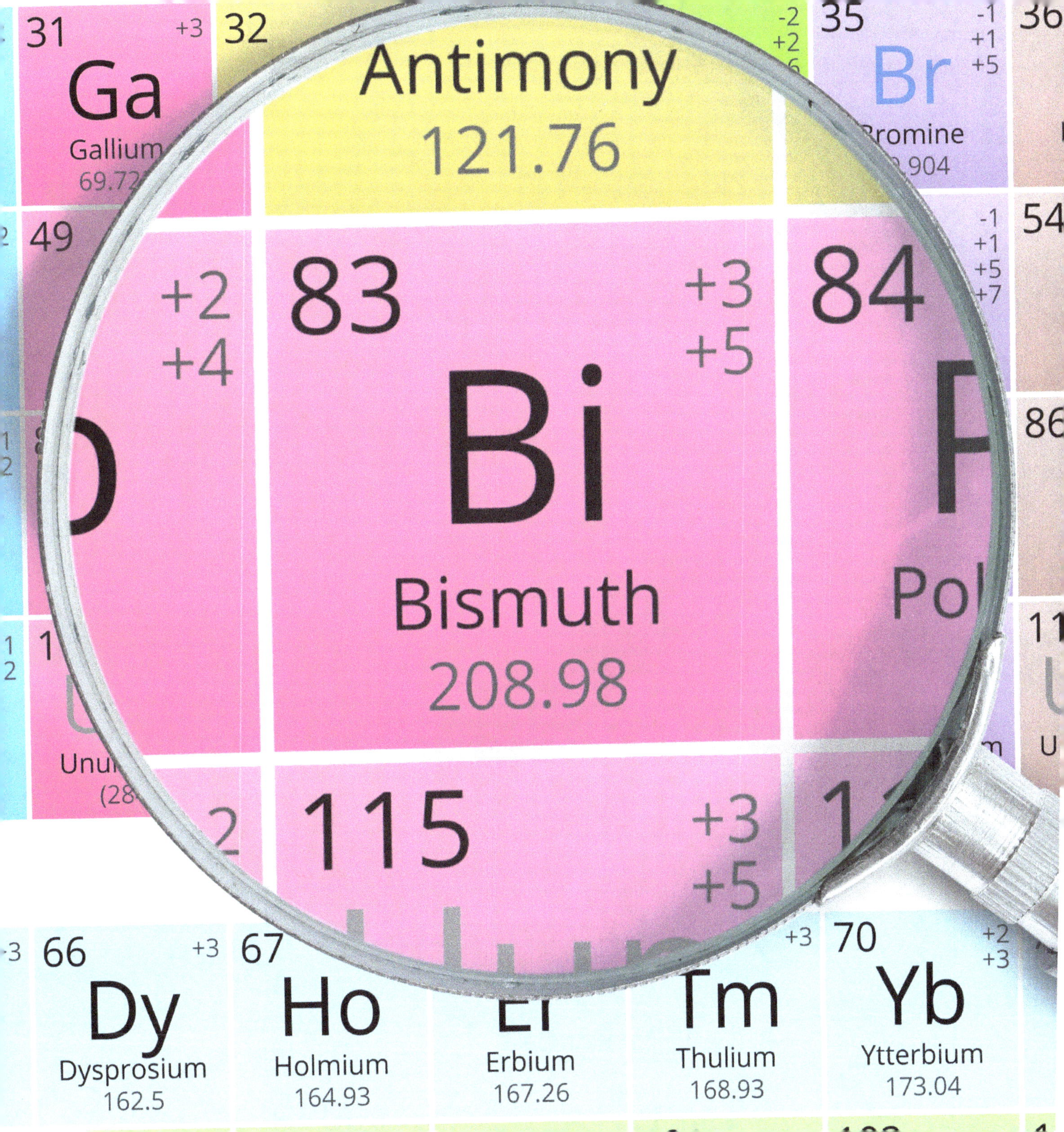
31
+3
Ga
Gallium
69.723
32
Antimony
121.76
35
-2
+2
6
-1
+1
+5
Br
Bromine
.904
36
49
+2
+4
83
+3
+5
Bi
Bismuth
208.98
84
-1
+1
+5
+7
P
Po
86
115
+3
+5
66
+3
Dy
Dysprosium
162.5
67
Ho
Holmium
164.93
Er
Erbium
167.26
+3
Tm
Thulium
168.93
70
+2
+3
Yb
Ytterbium
173.04

NONMETALS
ENS
GASES
13
IIIA
14
IVA
15
VA
16
VIA
Aluminium
26.982
-4
+2
7
N
Nitrogen
007
-3
-2
-1
+1
+2
+3
+4
8
O
Oxygen
15.999
-2
+2
31
Ga
Gallium
69.723
+3
32
-3
+3
+5
16
S
Sulfur
32.065
-2
+4
+6
34
Se
Selenium
78.96
Ger
52
Te
Tellurium
127.6
49
Au
Gold
196.97
+3
Mercury
200.59
Lead
207.2
Bi
Bismuth
208.98
112
113
114
115
116

WHICH POST-TRANSITION METAL IS MOST ABUNDANT?

Aluminum is the most abundant of the post-transition metals. It's also the metal that's most abundant in the crust of our planet. Gallium, is next in terms of abundance, followed by the elements of lead, tin, thallium, and indium. Bismuth is available in the least amounts.

INTERESTING FACTS ABOUT METALS LABELED POST-TRANSITION

- The element of zinc, the element of cadmium, and the element of mercury are sometimes organized with the metals labeled post-transition and sometimes organized with the metals labeled transition.

- After oxygen and silicon, aluminum is the third most abundant element in our planet's crust.

- Pepto-Bismol, which is a drug used to sooth upset stomachs, contains the element of bismuth.

- Indium is used in making electronics such as panel displays and other tablet screens.

- The name of thallium originates from the Greek word "thallos." Thallos means a "green twig." Thallium is very toxic and it can cause hair loss followed by death.

METALS
13 IIIA
14 IVA
15 VA
16 VIA
5
Silicon
28.086
-3
-2
8
O
Oxygen
999
9
F
17
+3
32
-4
+2
+4
Ge
Germanium
72.64
33
A
35
A
+1
+2
a
+1
48
+1
80
+1
+3
Hg
Mercury
200.59
50
+2
+4
53
-2
+4
+6
Cadm
112.
Thallium
204.38
smuth
208.98
+2
Po
Polonium
(209)
112
113
+1
114
+2
115
+3
116
+2

34

P

Se

Selenium
78.96
[Ar]3d

52

Te

35

B

Bromi

53

METALLOIDS

The metalloids are a group of elements in the periodic table. They are located in a step-like line between the metals and non-metals. Metalloids, which include arsenic, antimony, boron, germanium, silicon, and tellurium, share some properties with non-metals and metals. The elements selenium and polonium are sometimes considered to be metalloids as well.

WHAT PROPERTIES DO METALLOIDS HAVE IN COMMON?

Even though metalloids are similar to metals in appearance, they are much more brittle. They can combine with metals to form alloys. Under standard conditions, the elements of silicon and germanium are solid, but under special conditions, they become excellent conductors of electricity. They are called semiconductors for this reason. They are considered to behave like nonmetallic elements in their chemical behavior.

silicon
14
Si
28.086
phospho
15
P
30.9
germa
32
arse
3
14.007

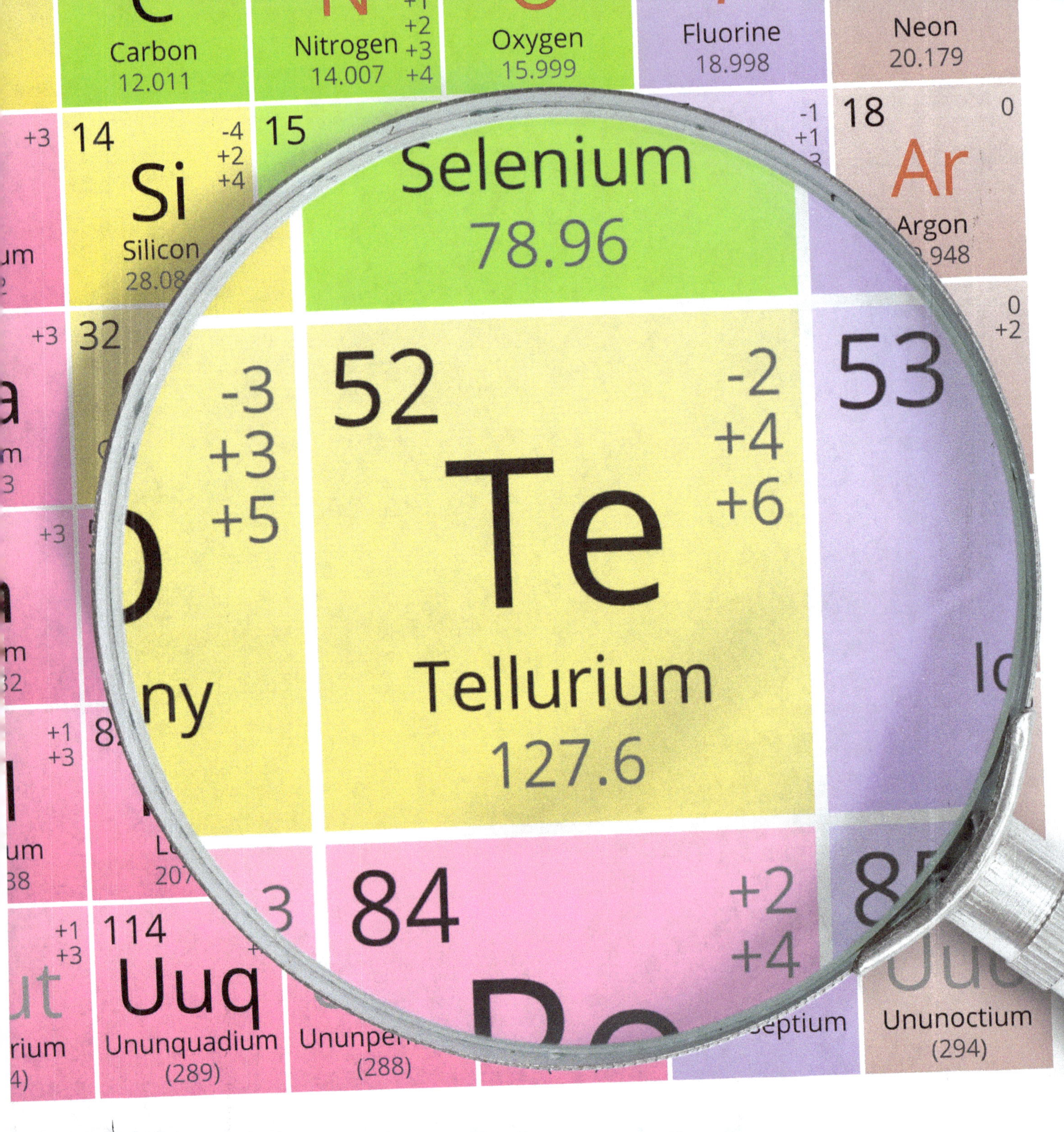
Carbon
12.011
Nitrogen
14.007
Oxygen
15.999
Fluorine
18.998
Neon
20.179
Selenium
78.96
Ar
Argon
Si
Silicon
28.08
52
Te
Tellurium
127.6
53
Uuq
Ununquadium
(289)
Ununpe
(288)
84
Ununoctium
(294)

WHICH METALLOIDS ARE THE MOST ABUNDANT?

After oxygen, silicon is the most abundant element in the Earth's crust. The least abundant of the metalloids is tellurium. It is a very rare stable element, similar in abundance to platinum. If you were to measure the metalloids in the Earth's crust, you would find silicon to be the most dominant, followed by boron, then germanium, arsenic, antimony, and tellurium.

INTERESTING FACTS ABOUT METALLOIDS

• Most of the other groups of elements form vertical lines, but the metalloids form a "staircase" diagonal line in the table.

• Silicon Valley gets its name from silicon, which is used to make electronics, such as smart phones, computers, and tablets.

• Arsenic is a very poisonous element.

• The elements of antimony and tellurium are used to make alloys.

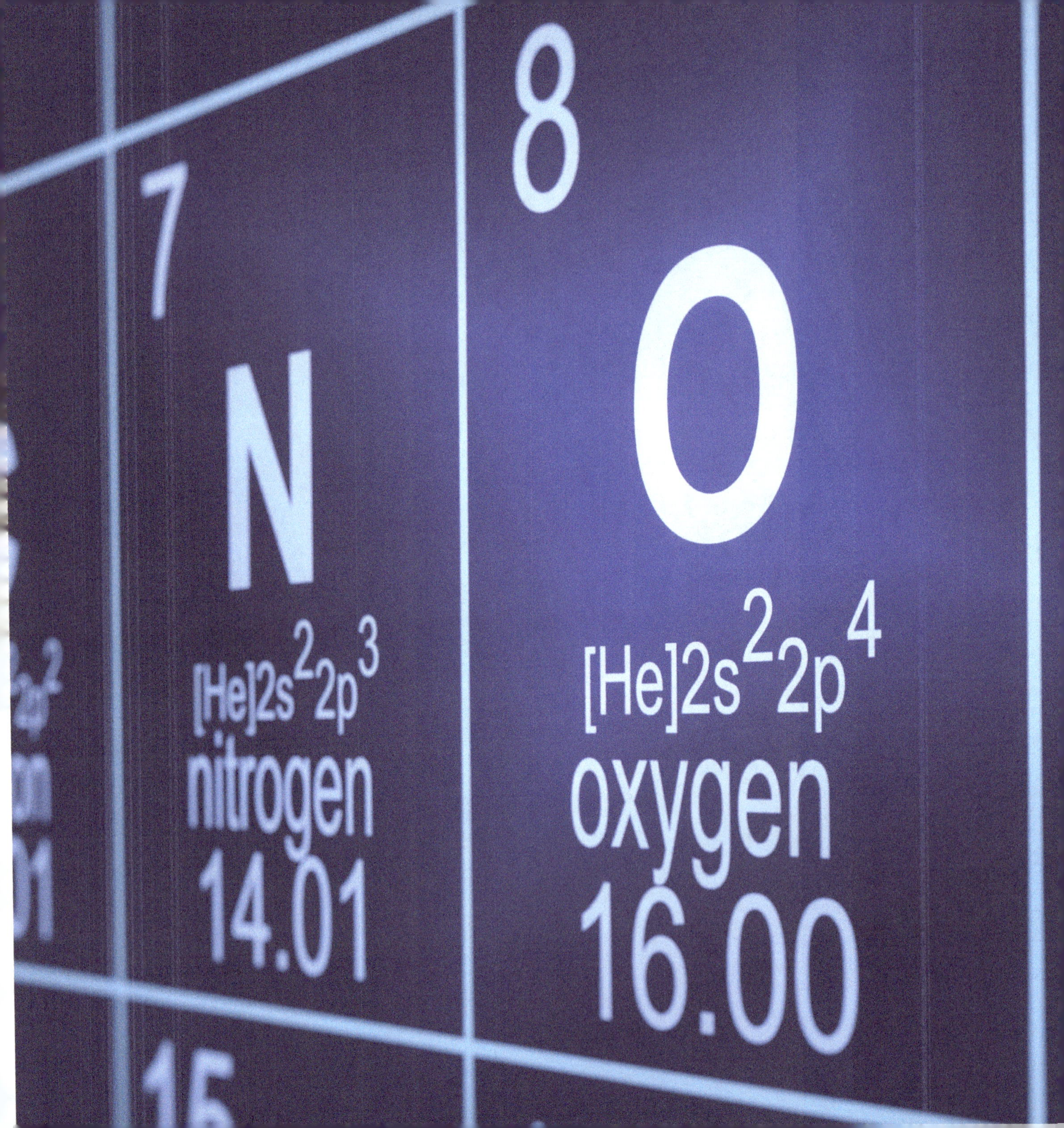

7
N
[He]2s^{2}2p^3
nitrogen
14.01

8
O
[He]2s^{2}2p^4
oxygen
16.00

15

NONMETALS

Another group in the periodic table is the nonmetals. In the table, they are located left of the halogens and to the right of the metalloids. Since noble gases and halogens are also nonmetals, these elements are often referred to as "other nonmetals." These elements are very common throughout the Earth and our entire universe. They're even inside our own bodies.

WHICH ELEMENTS ARE NONMETALS?

The "other nonmetals" include the seven elements of carbon, hydrogen, nitrogen, oxygen, phosphorus, sulfur, and selenium. The subgroup pnictogens includes phosphorus and nitrogen, and the subgroup chalcogens which also includes oxygen, selenium, and sulfur nitrogen.

7
Nitrogen
N
14.0067

8
Oxygen
O
15.9994

9
Fluorine
F
18.9984

12
Magnesium
Mg
24.305

11
Sodium
Na
22.9897

10
Neon
Ne
20.1797

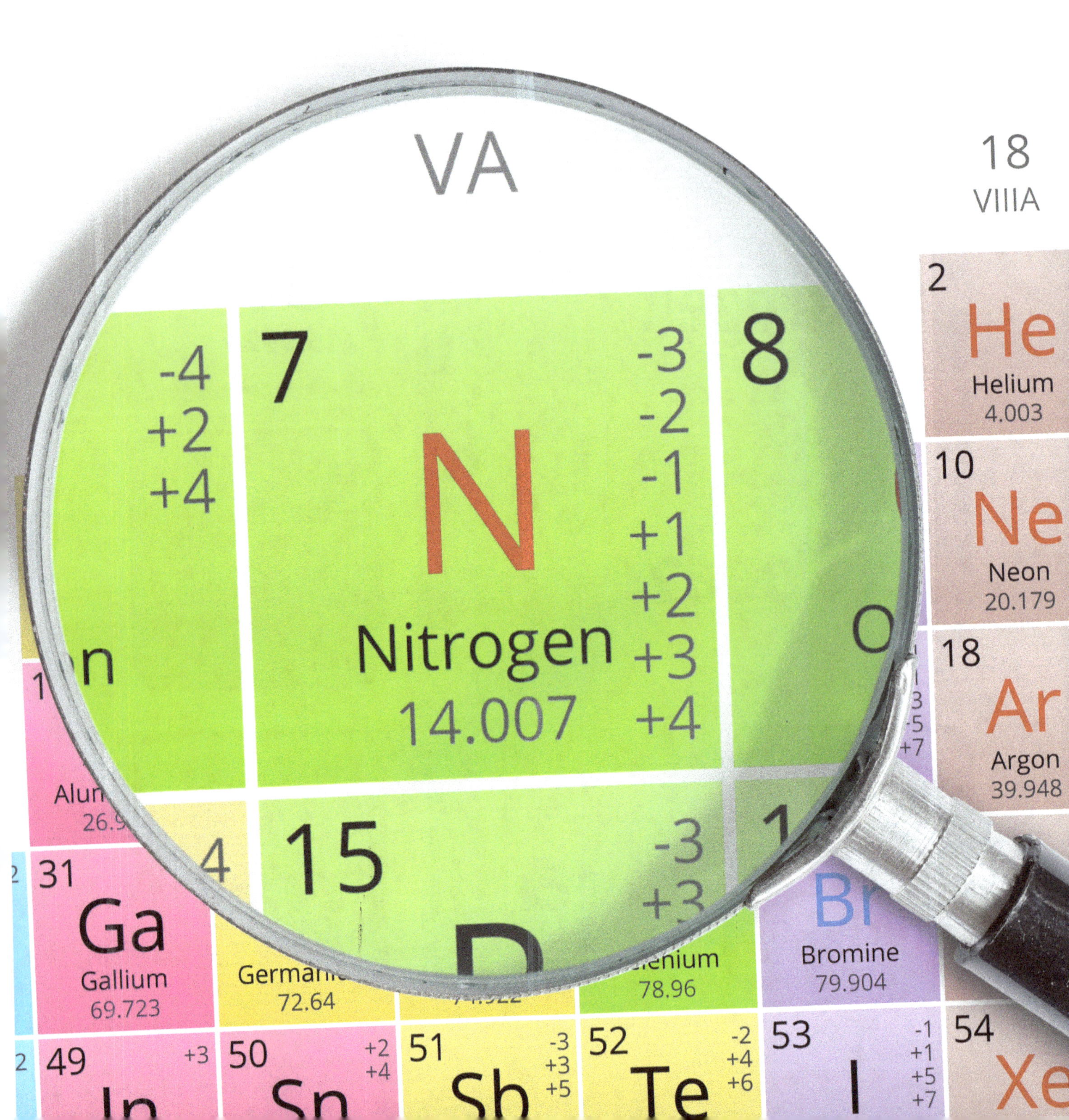

VA
18
VIIIA
-4
+2
+4
7
-3
-2
-1
+1
+2
+3
+4
N
Nitrogen
14.007
8
O
2
He
Helium
4.003
10
Ne
Neon
20.179
18
Ar
Argon
39.948
n
Alum
26.9
31
Ga
Gallium
69.723
4
15
P
-3
+3
Germani
72.64
enium
78.96
1
Bromine
79.904
Br
49
In
50
Sn
+2
+4
51
Sb
-3
+3
+5
52
Te
-2
+4
+6
53
I
-1
+1
+5
+7
54
Xe

WHAT PROPERTIES DO NONMETALS HAVE IN COMMON?

Under standard conditions, they are either gas, such as hydrogen, or solid, such as carbon. They're NOT good conductors of either electricity or heat. Unlike metals, they are very brittle and they have lower densities. They are not ductile or malleable. Other than carbon, they have lower points for both melting and boiling. Their ionization energies are high.

WHICH NONMETALS ARE THE MOST ABUNDANT?

Hydrogen is the most abundant element in the universe. Earth's atmosphere is made up of nitrogen and oxygen with nitrogen around 80% and oxygen around 20%.

7
N
[He]2s² 2p³
nitrogen
14.01
8
O
[He]2s² 2p⁴
oxygen
16.00
9

H₂O

By mass, the most abundant elements in the human body are oxygen, carbon, hydrogen, and nitrogen.

INTERESTING FACTS ABOUT NONMETALS

• Water is made up of molecules of oxygen and hydrogen.

• Even if you count the noble gases and the halogens, only 18 elements in the table are nonmetals.

• Under very high pressures, some of the nonmetals behave more like metals.

• Carbon is the most important element to all life forms on Earth.

C
C

PERIODIC TABLE OF THE ELEMENTS
Long Shadow Style

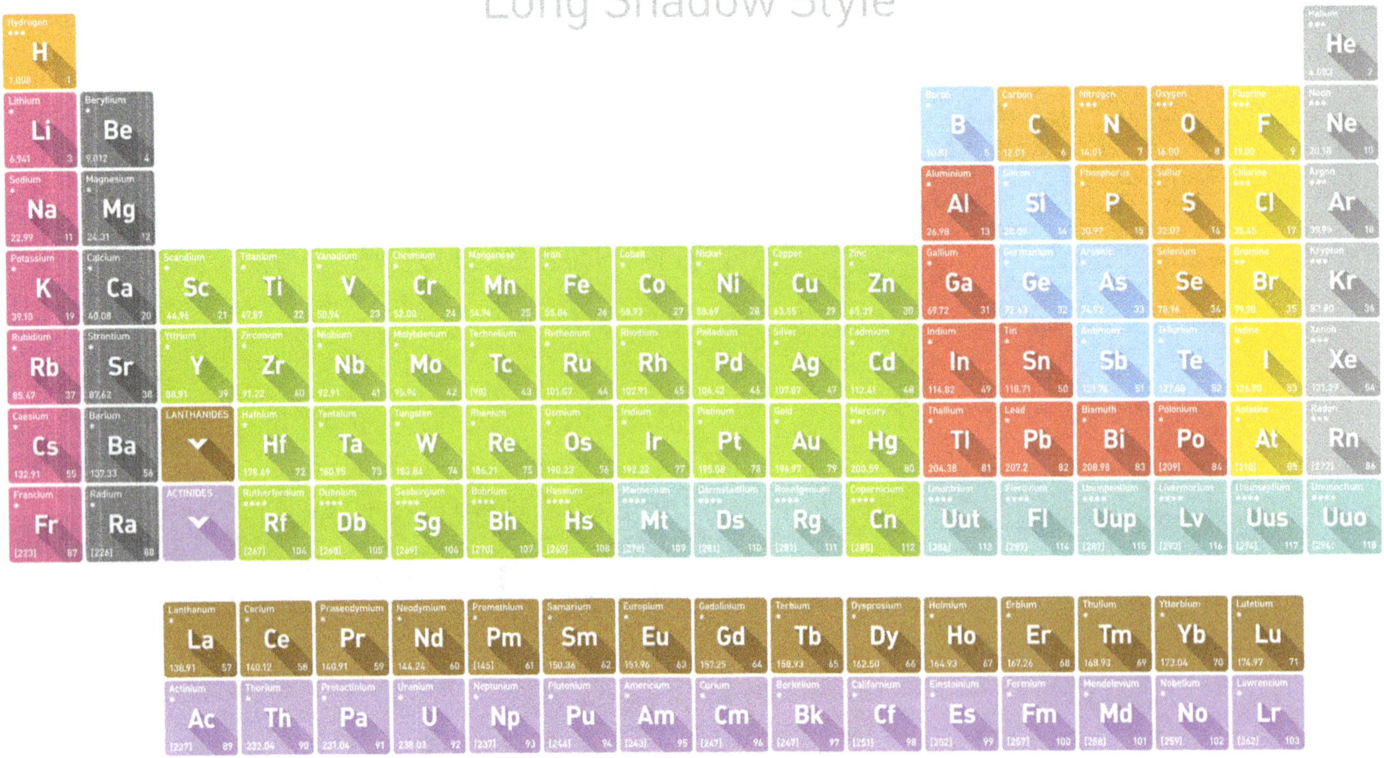

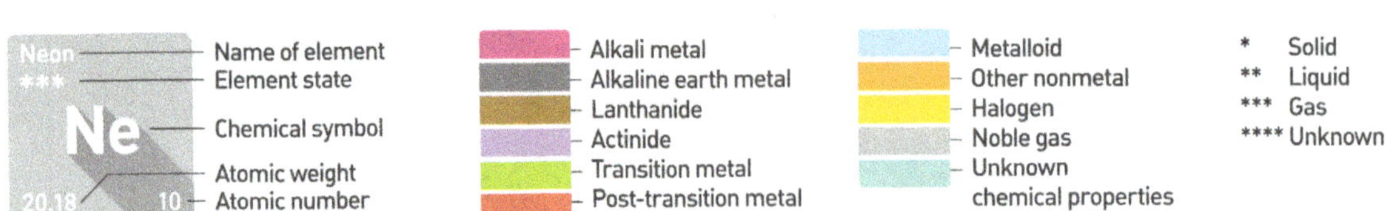

Awesome! Now that you've read this book you know more about Chemistry and the Periodic Table. You can find more Chemistry books from Baby Professor by searching the website of your favorite book retailer.

Visit
BABY PROFESSOR
EDUCATION KIDS
www.BabyProfessorBooks.com
to download Free Baby Professor eBooks
and view our catalog of new and exciting
Children's Books